Lives and Times

Scott Joplin

The King of Ragtime

Jennifer Blizin Gillis

Heinemann Library
Chicago, Illinois

© 2006 Heinemann Library
a division of Reed Elsevier Inc.
Chicago, Illinois

Customer Service 888-454-2279
Visit our website at www.heinemannlibrary.com

Designed by Lucy Owen and Bridge Creative Services
Originated by Modern Age Repro
Printed and bound by South China Printing Company

10 09 08
10 9 8 7 6 5 4 3 2

Library of Congress Cataloging-in-Publication Data
Gillis, Jennifer Blizin, 1950-
  Scott Joplin : ragtime legend / Jennifer Blizin Gillis.
    p. cm. -- (Lives and times)
  Includes bibliographical references and index.
  ISBN 1-4034-6749-8 (library binding-hardcover)
  ISBN 978-1-4034-6749-2 (HC)
  ISBN 978-1-4034-6757-7 (Pbk.)
  1. Joplin, Scott, 1868-1917--Juvenile literature. 2.
Composers--United States--Biography--Juvenile
literature. I. Title. II. Series: Lives and times (Des
Plaines, Ill.)
  ML3930.J66G55 2005
  780'.92--dc22
                                    2005001497

Acknowledgments
The author and publishers are grateful to the following
for permission to reproduce copyright material:
Alamy p. **8**; Corbis pp. **11, 22**; Corbis/Bettmann p. **14**;
Edward A. Berlin pp. **17, 19, 20, 23**; Fisk University
Special Collections p. **16**; Getty Images/Hulton Archive
pp. **12, 18, 24**; Image Works p. **27**; Lebrecht Music
Collection p. **5**; Peter Newark's Americana Library
pp. **4, 6**; Rosalind Hudson pp. **9, 15**; Scott Joplin
Museum pp. **13, 21, 25**; The Kobal Collection p. **26**;
The Library of Congress pp. **7, 10**.

Cover photograph of Scott Joplin reproduced with
permission of Getty News & Sport. Photograph of
music manuscript reproduced with permission of
Corbis.

Page icons by Getty Images/Photodisc

Photo research by Maria Joannou and Virginia
Stroud-Lewis

Every effort has been made to contact copyright
holders of any material reproduced in this book.
Any omissions will be rectified in subsequent
printings if notice is given to the publishers.

Contents

Some words are shown in bold, **like this**. You can find out what they mean by looking in the glossary.

The King of Ragtime

Scott Joplin was an African-American **musician**. In the 1900s he helped **invent** a kind of music called "ragtime." It mixed African-American music with marches and other kinds of tunes.

There are few pictures of Scott. This one was taken when he was about 36 years old.

The United States Postal Service made this stamp of Scott in 1983.

When Scott was alive, African Americans and white people did not do things together. But Scott wrote many songs that were popular with everyone. People called him the "King of Ragtime."

A Musical Family

Scott was probably born in 1868 in Texas. In those days people often did not write down birth dates. Scott's mother, Florence, was from Kentucky. Scott's father, Giles, had been a **slave** in North Carolina.

People who had been slaves could not afford to buy a house. Instead they built houses out of whatever they could find.

During their free time, people often got together and played music.

Scott's mother played the banjo. His father played the violin. They taught Scott and his brothers to play. If Scott heard a tune once, he could play it perfectly.

Learning About Music

There were few schools for African Americans. Scott learned to read and write from **tutors**. He took music lessons, too. Soon he could make up his own songs.

Scott also learned to play a horn like this, called a cornet.

When Scott was about 12, his father left. Scott's mother had to clean houses to make money. One family let Scott play their piano while his mother cleaned their house.

The piano was Scott's favorite instrument.

Earning a Living

Scott's mother wanted him to get a job. But there were few good jobs for African Americans in those days. In most places they were not treated well. Scott decided to play music to make money.

Most jobs for African Americans were hard or dangerous.

There were many bands like Scott's.

Scott started a band with his brothers, Will and Robert. It was called the Texas **Medley Quartet**. Scott played the piano. They made money playing music for dances.

Leaving Home

When Scott was about 20, he left home. He played piano in **saloons** all around the Midwest. New towns opened up as people moved west. Each new town had at least one saloon.

Scott learned all kinds of music when he worked in saloons like this one.

Scott moved to St. Louis, Missouri, when he was about 22. He got a job playing the piano in a saloon. His friend Tom's family owned the saloon. Scott moved in with them.

This is Scott's friend, Tom Turpin.

A New Sound

About three years later, Scott went to Chicago. There was a World's Fair there. There were exhibits from many countries. He met **musicians** from Africa. He heard many different kinds of music.

People from all over the world came to Chicago for the World's Fair, called the Columbian **Exposition**.

Scott went to work in **saloons** near the
fair. He began to write piano music. His
left hand played a marching beat. His
right hand played a different beat. Scott's
friends called this music "ragtime."

People liked hearing Scott's
ragtime music in saloons.

Sedalia

Soon Scott moved to Sedalia, Missouri. There was a large African-American community there. For the first time, Scott lived with African-American people who owned businesses and lived in nice houses.

Scott got a job playing in this marching band in Sedalia.

The first song Scott published was "Please Say You Will."

Scott played piano in some clubs. He started up the Texas **Medley Quartet** again. His brothers, Will and Robert, came to join the band. Then Scott began **publishing** his music.

17

Success!

Scott **published** a song called "Maple Leaf Rag" when he was about 31 years old. In 6 months he sold 75,000 copies. Soon he was the most popular ragtime songwriter in the country.

In Scott's time playing the piano was a popular hobby. This is sheet music for "Maple Leaf Rag."

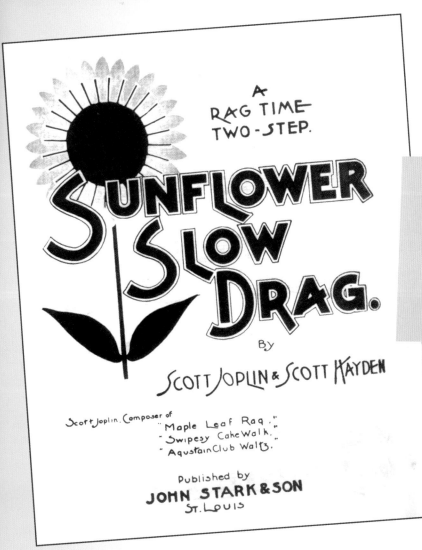

This is the sheet music for a song that Scott Joplin wrote with Scott Hayden.

That same year he wrote a song with a **musician** named Scott Hayden, who had a sister named Belle. Scott Joplin and Belle fell in love. They were married the next year.

Sad Times

Scott and Belle had a daughter in 1902, but she died after a few months. Belle and Scott got divorced. Then, Scott found out that his brother Will had died.

Scott Joplin.

This is a picture of Scott from a newspaper article about him.

Some people think this may be a picture of Freddie Alexander.

The next year Scott met a girl named Freddie Alexander. They married, but Freddie got very sick. She died after just a few weeks. Some people think Scott never got over her death.

New York City

Scott moved to New York when he was about 39 years old. He became well known for the music he wrote. He wrote a book called *School of Ragtime*. It taught people how to play ragtime piano.

Scott lived near Broadway in New York City. There were many theaters and clubs there.

Most people did not think of ragtime as important music. But Scott wanted people to take it seriously. He began writing a ragtime **opera**. It was called *Treemonisha*. Some people think it was about his wife, Freddie.

Scott sent this form to the government to get a **copyright** for his opera.

Last Years

Scott worked so hard on his opera that he stopped writing other music. He tried to get his opera into a theater. But no one was interested in it. He ran out of money.

This is how Scott looked toward the end of his life.

Scott was buried in St. Michael's Cemetery on Long Island, New York.

Little by little Scott had been getting sick. By the time he was 47, he could hardly play the piano. Two years later, he had to go into a hospital. He died there on April 1, 1917.

Learning More About Scott Joplin

After Scott died people forgot about his music. A new kind of music called jazz became popular. But in the 1940s some **musicians** began playing Scott's music again. People loved it!

Ragtime became more popular in the 1970s when a movie called *The Sting* used one of Scott's songs, called "The Entertainer."

This is a performance of *Treemonisha*.

In 1975 Scott's **opera** *Treemonisha* was performed on Broadway in New York. Sixty years after Scott died, he won an important prize for his music.

Fact File

- Scott had three brothers named Monroe, Will, and Robert, and two sisters named Myrtle and Ossie.

- Scott was always very quiet and shy. His friends said he never talked or smiled very much.

- One of Scott's first music teachers was a German **immigrant** named Julius Weiss. He taught Scott to love classical music and **opera**.

- Scott wrote more than 70 ragtime tunes during his lifetime. He also wrote marches and waltzes.

- Many people think that Scott's most famous song, "The Maple Leaf Rag," was named for an African-American club in Sedalia, Missouri, called "The Maple Leaf Club."

Timeline

about 1868 Scott is born
about 1880 Scott's father moves away
about 1888 Scott leaves home and travels the Midwest
about 1890 Scott moves to St. Louis, Missouri
about 1894 Scott moves to Sedalia, Missouri
1895 Scott **publishes** his first song
1899 Scott publishes "The Maple Leaf Rag"
1900 Scott marries Belle Hayden
1903 Scott and Belle divorce
1904 Scott marries Freddie Alexander
1907 Scott moves to New York City
1911 Scott publishes *Treemonisha*
1915 Scott begins getting sick
1917 Scott dies on April 1

Glossary

copyright to register something you have written with the government so that no one else can make money from it

exposition very large fair

immigrant person who leaves one country to live in another country

invent to come up with the idea for a new thing

medley piece of music made up of many different songs

musician person who plays music

opera play in which performers sing their parts

publish have something printed so that it can be sold to other people

quartet musical group made up of four people

saloon kind of large room where people can listen to music, eat, and drink

slave person who is owned by another person and must do work for him or her

tutor teacher who gives lessons at a student's home

Find Out More

More Books to Read

An older reader can help you with these books:

Bankston, John. *The Life and Times of Scott Joplin.* Hockessin, Del.: Mitchell Lane, 2004.

Preston, Katherine. *Scott Joplin.* New York, N.Y.: Chelsea House, 1988.

Sabir, C. Ogbu. *Scott Joplin: The King of Ragtime.* Chanhassen, Minn.: Child's World, 2000.

Places to Visit

You can visit the apartment where Scott and Belle lived, which features an exhibit about Scott:

Scott Joplin House
2658A Delmar Boulevard
St. Louis, Missouri 63103
(314) 340-5790

You can learn about Scott at this museum:

Texarkana Museum of Regional History
219 N. State Line Avenue
Texarkana, Texas 75501
(903) 793-4831

Index